mini
EXPLORERS

Horses

Written by: Kirsty Neale
Illustrated by: Matthew Williams

A Horse at Home

Many ponies can live outdoors all year round, but horses need the shelter of a stable at night. They also need a large field to run around in during the day.

Horses often exercise in a covered area called a school or ménage. It has a hard surface, and can be used for indoor jumping.

A male horse is called a stallion, a

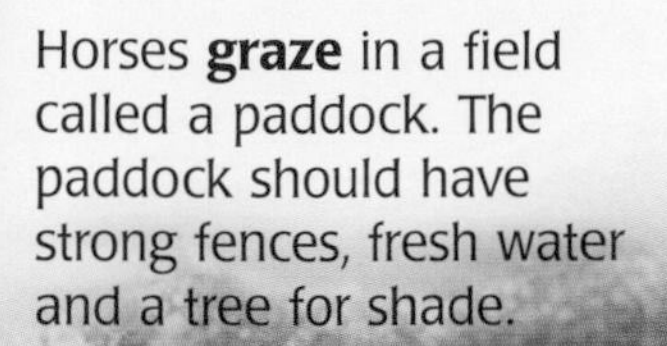

Horses **graze** in a field called a paddock. The paddock should have strong fences, fresh water and a tree for shade.

The stable

The half-doors in a stable give horses plenty of fresh air. Inside, they have **hay** to eat, and a bucket of water. Once a day, droppings and wet straw are **mucked out**.

Parts of a Horse

Horses and ponies come in all shapes and sizes. The different parts of a horse have special names.

▼ Bay is the most common horse's coat, but coats can also be other shades of brown, black, grey, white or cream.

Horses measure 14.2 hands or taller,

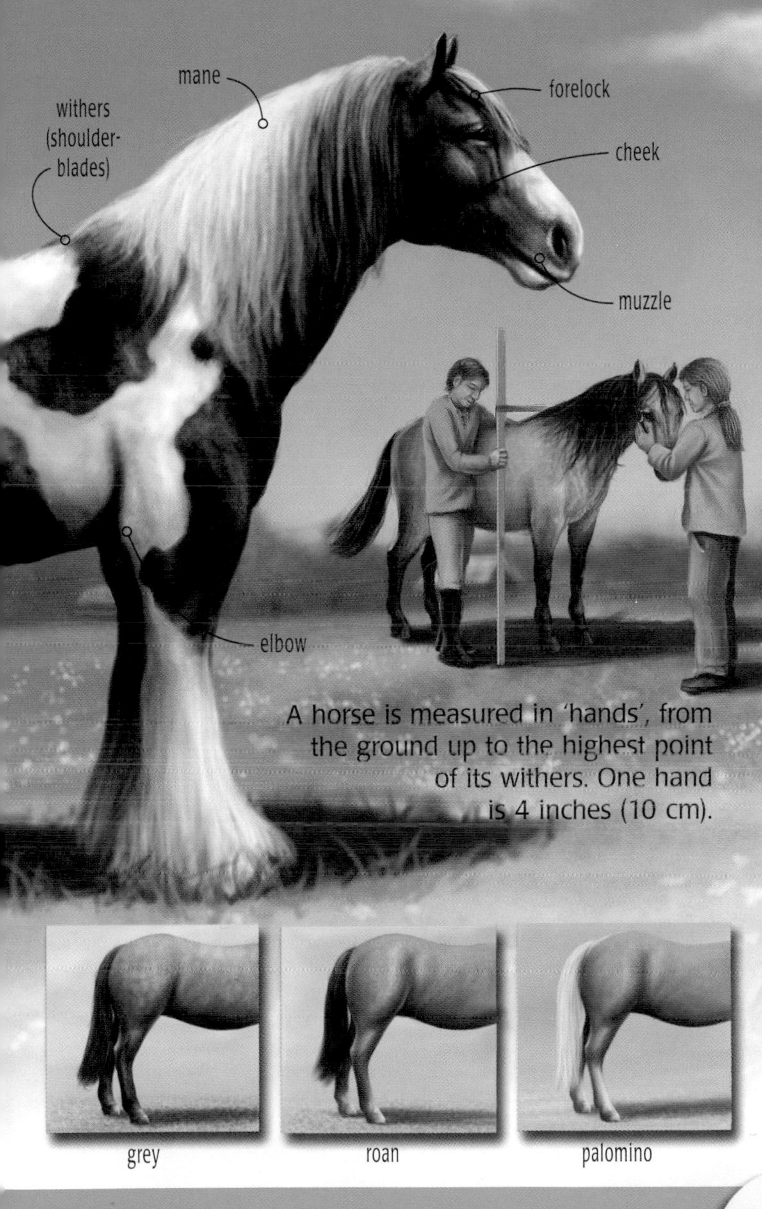

A horse is measured in 'hands', from the ground up to the highest point of its withers. One hand is 4 inches (10 cm).

and ponies are less than 14.2 hands.

Grooming and Care

Grooming keeps a horse's coat clean and healthy. It's a good way for a rider to make friends with a horse. A careful owner grooms their horse every day.

Riders often plait, or braid, their horse's mane and tail for shows and competitions. Some even fix the braids in place with hairspray and gel!

A horse's metal shoes are made by a

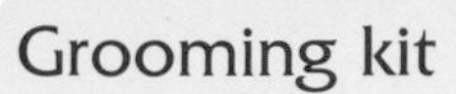

Grooming kit

A **dandy brush** has stiff bristles that remove dirt and dust. A **body brush** and sponges are more gentle. The curry comb is used to clean the other brushes.

curry comb

dandy brushes

body brush

sponges

A show horse often has a pattern, called a **quarter mark**, on its hindquarters. It's made by brushing and combing the hair in different directions.

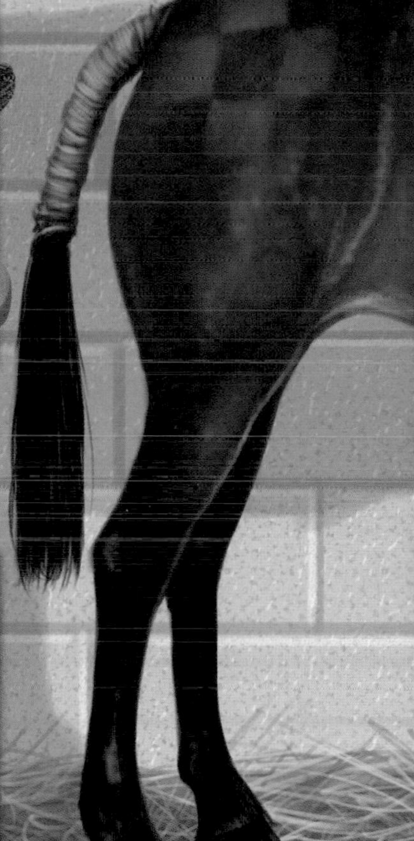

A hoof pick is used to scrape out dirt and stones from the underside of a horse's hooves.

blacksmith and fitted by a farrier.

Horses through History

Horses have lived and worked alongside people for thousands of years. Since ancient times, they've been used by farmers and soldiers, as well as being ridden by explorers, hunters and sportspeople.

Many people today enjoy watching horses race around a flat track, or over jumps. **Dressage** and show-jumping are also popular sporting events, and form part of the Olympic Games.

The world's fastest horses race at

In Roman times, horses were used to pull two-wheeled chariots in exciting races, battles or grand processions.

Draft horses were once commonly used on farms to pull carts and machinery. They still do this in some parts of the world.

Medieval knights rode their warhorses into battle and held mock fights in jousting tournaments.

Before trains or cars were invented, horse-drawn carriages carried people around cities and from town to town.

speeds of 55 mph (89 km/h).

Different Kinds of Horses

A breed is a group of horses with similar looks and skills. These could be size, shape, speed or strength. If the parents of a horse are both the same breed, the horse is known as a purebred, or thoroughbred.

Shetland ponies are very small, but strong for their size. They have thick coats and can live outdoors all year round.

Lipizzaner horses are known for their dressage skills. Many are trained at the famous **Spanish Riding School** of Vienna, in Austria.

There are more than 300 different

The wild mustang horse was brought to America by the Spanish. Native Americans learned how to catch and ride them.

The Arab, or Arabian, horse is an old breed known for its intelligence. Arab horses have big eyes, flaring nostrils and a high tail.

Shire horses once pulled carts delivering beer. Today, they are often seen carrying drums in official processions.

breeds of horse in the world today.

Horse Talk

Horses are sensitive animals. They're easily startled, and will run away in fright. It's important for a rider to understand why a horse behaves the way it does.

▼ A horse and rider have to trust each other. A horse that follows its rider without being led is showing complete trust in the person.

A horse will often greet its rider with a **whinny**. If it snorts or sneezes, it is showing that it is happy to do as it is being told.

Horses are very sensitive to the tone

In the wild, horses live in a **herd**. They like to be with other horses, and enjoy running and playing together.

▶ When a horse is relaxed, its lower lip hangs down and its ears point out to the sides.

of voice in which a command is given.

Bridle and Saddle

The equipment used for riding a horse is called tack. It includes saddles, stirrups, bridles, **bits** and reins. Fitting tack on to a horse is called tacking up, and the equipment is kept in a tack room.

browband
headpiece
noseband
throatlash
cheekpiece
reins
bit

A rider uses a set of leather straps called a bridle to help control a horse. Reins are attached to the metal bit, which goes inside the horse's mouth.

Saddles and bridles are washed with

The saddle is a leather seat, held in place by a strap called a girth or cinch, which passes under the horse's belly. Stirrups support the rider's feet.

Riding gear

A rider's outfit includes jodhpurs, which are made from stretchy fabric so the rider can move easily, and tough, low-heeled boots. The most important piece of equipment is a hard riding hat, or helmet, for safety.

a special cleaner called saddle-soap.

How to Ride a Horse

A horse can walk slowly, speed up to a trot and move even faster when it canters or gallops. The rider instructs the horse with words and noises, and by gently squeezing its body with his or her legs.

▼ Walking is a horse's slowest speed. The rider sways from side to side as the horse moves along.

To get on, or mount, a horse, the rider puts one foot into a stirrup and swings the other foot over the horse's back.

At one hour old, a foal can stand, and

Trotting is bumpy for the rider. To make it easier, the person can rise up and sit down as the horse trots along.

When a horse canters, or lopes, it moves quite quickly. The rider sits still and straight, with relaxed arms and short reins.

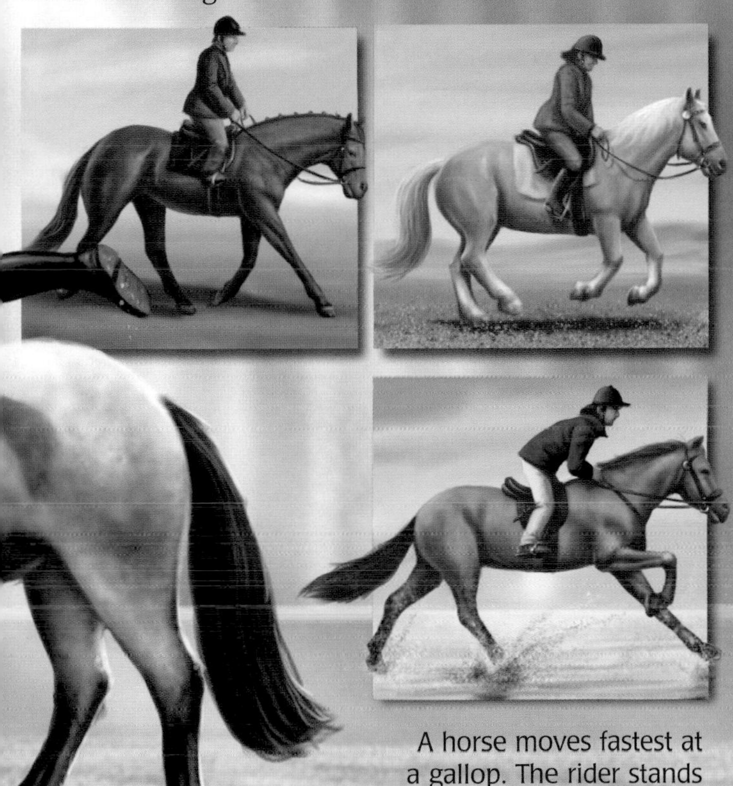

A horse moves fastest at a gallop. The rider stands up in the stirrups and leans forward over the horse's neck.

after two hours it can walk, trot and run.

Fun at the Show

Horses and riders can have lots of fun at a show! It's a great place for a rider to learn new skills and enjoy spending time with their horse and with friends.

Often at a show, horses do fancy

▼ A horse is taken to a show in a horse box. Special clothes and equipment protect it from knocks and bumps.

◀ The winning show-jumper is the horse that goes over the most jumps in the fastest time and makes the fewest mistakes.

▲ A show may include a fancy-dress competition. Riders dress up in costume, and their horses are often decorated, too!

footwork exercises, called dressage.

Glossary

Bit
A metal bar attached to the bridle and reins. It rests inside the horse's mouth. The rider is able to control the horse by putting gentle pressure on its gums.

Body brush
A body brush is used to smooth down a horse's hair after the dirt has been removed.

Dandy brush
A 'flicking' action is needed when using a dandy brush, away and up from the horse's coat. Dirt should come away in a slight cloud of dust with each stroke.

Dressage
Horse-training and exercises in which the rider guides the horse using slight movements of his or her hands, legs and weight.

Farrier
Originally a farrier was a horse doctor, but now it means someone who puts shoes on a horse.

Graze
To eat grass.

Grooming
Cleaning, brushing and taking care of a horse. The horse should be brushed from the top of its neck towards its tail, on both sides. Special care must be taken when grooming its face. For safety, a horse should be tied up while it is being groomed.

Hay
Cut and dried grass, fed to a horse when there is not enough grass for grazing, such as in the winter or when the animal is being kept indoors in its stable.

Herd
A group of horses, usually in the wild. The head of a herd is usually an older female, or 'boss' mare.

Mucking out
The daily removal of droppings and wet straw from a horse's stable.

Quarter mark
A decorative marking brushed into a horse's coat. It draws attention to the good condition of a show horse's coat, which should be clean and shiny.

Spanish Riding School
Founded in 1572, the Spanish Riding School in Vienna is the oldest riding school of its kind in the world. It teaches dressage.

Whinny
The soft, neighing sound that a horse makes.